Praise for

THE SECRETS TO WHAT MEN

"Lisa Palmer is the cupid-of-millionaires."

—Piers Morgan

"Lisa that was mesmerizing."

—Simon Cowell

"This is such a great read! Comical whilst answering all those questions that many of us are often too scared to ask! I've no doubt that this book will set many people on the right path to finally finding love or helping those to rekindle their romance who have already been lucky enough to find Mr. Right! Well done, Lisa!"

—Natalie Graham, Music Manager & BBC Radio Presenter

"Lisa is a long-term acquaintance of mine as we both networked the luxury events of London and we've enjoyed many a fine Champagne-tasting event. Her desire to explore what attracts men even led us to do a private tasting to see if the smell of Champagne on a lady's skin could attract!

"Her bubbly personality and dedication to her subject shines through in this book. It's a fun read, engages your mind and at the same times delivers an education that I'm sure still puzzles many. Well done, Lisa!"

—Christopher Walkey, Champagne and sparkling wine correspondent, UK's Champagne ambassador

The Secrets to What Men Really Want

by Lisa Palmer

ISBN 978-1-64663-122-3

Published by

köehlerbooks™

210 60th Street
Virginia Beach, VA 23451
800–435–4811
www.koehlerbooks.com

THE
SECRETS
TO WHAT MEN
—— *Really* ——
WANT

LISA PALMER
THE MOGUL MATCHMAKER

VIRGINIA BEACH
CAPE CHARLES

TABLE OF CONTENTS

FOREWORD IX
INTRODUCTION 1

1. THE FIRST DATE AND YOUR NEW
POWER TEAM:
Me, the Police, Fire and Ambulance Service 3

2. MAKEUP FOR A FIRST DATE AND
WHAT TO WEAR 12

3. HOW TO FLIRT
The Lady and the Guy with the Humongous Balls 16

4. DATING AND FINDING COMMON GROUND AND
THINGS YOU BOTH ENJOY
The Story of "A Wee-ly Nice Bloke,
but It All Went Wrong." 21

5. WHAT TO SAY ON A DATE AND THE RIGHT BODY
LANGUAGE; CONFIDENCE AND HOW TO TELL HE IS
BEING TRUTHFUL
"My New Hubby Had No Penis" 26

6. WHAT MEN REALLY WANT AND
HOW TO KEEP HIM
Mary Poppins and the Whore......................31

7. WHAT TO DO TO TURN HIM ON 35

8. HOW TO MAKE A MAN HAPPY................. 38
**The Story of the Lady "Who Would Rather
Cut Off Her Right Toe Than Give Him Another
Blow Job!"** 38

9. STALE RELATIONSHIPS
**How to Bring Back the Fun
and Keep the Romance Alive**.................... 42

ACKNOWLEDGMENTS........................... 45

FOREWORD

I am privileged to have known and worked with the inspirational author, life coach, and internationally acclaimed dating expert Lisa Palmer. In a world of fake identities, letdowns, lies, and the ultimate deception, dating has become, for millions of guys around the world, a huge enigmatic process. Who can we trust, and how long might it last? In a world of dangerous personalities, many guys want the best partner that is reasonably possible with socially compatible personality traits and a relationship that will ultimately be positively rewarding and fulfilling.

As a British ex academic who has taught the science of love, sex, and attraction for a few decades in British universities, and now working in celebrity culture, I have reviewed a plethora of textbooks on love and attraction. Most of them boast expertise which, with my critical eye, is invariably devoid of honesty and authenticity. Theories in social psychology are only theories at the end of the day. Academics live in academia and do help us to understand the facts of the matter with regard to the principles of love, dating, and sexual relationships.

However, their models of interpersonal attraction can become questionable. When we get down to the social-psychological processes involved at the personal level, as we contemplate the huge investment involved in seeking a new potential lover and life partner, there is so much more involved, obliterated by the world's social psychologists, as we socially interact in a fast-paced society within and between cultures.

This book is ahead of its time. It is ecologically rich in its mind-absorbing content, with mind-boosting techniques on how to do the deal and achieve the man or woman of your dreams. After the first few chapters, I was acquiring well-tested techniques that I found rich, compelling, and highly unique. Lisa pulls no punches but tells you precisely what it says on the cover. She opens up a new world of genuine secrets of what men really do want, and it's not quite what you might think. Buy this brilliant book, digest its scientifically tested techniques based on pure authenticity. Avoid the anxiety of past relationships with those who might be paranoid, narcissistic, or who have been emotionally unstable. Lisa helps you to choose the right guy from the very basics of human love and attraction. I warmly commend this thrilling exciting and illuminating text to you.

Arthur Cassidy C.Psychol, Ph.D, AFBPsS
Celebrity Psychologist
London.

INTRODUCTION

L et's begin with this: It should be totally understood that, in my opinion, men are simple creatures, and the way to a man's heart is his belly, ego, (his) hobbies and his . . . you know—let's face it, girls, all of which need constant attention and your undying approval and support! We love them, but boy are they hard work sometimes.

So, why write a book? Well, the truth is, people have been asking me to do it for years, and now felt like the right time. I guess I can tell you how it really is. The reason I think my book is worth reading is simple: I am a qualified dating and relationship expert with the kind of experience that money can't buy! I'm the go-to girl you don't get access to.

I have worked with the rich, famous and, on occasion, infamous! I have appeared on mainstream TV, radio and have appeared in countless press articles.

What motivates and inspires me? The feedback from my extraordinary, talented, crazy, lovely clients that make my job the best in the world. After all, what price do you put on love?

The book is designed to do two things: (1) recognize where you are today and what you should do next if you are in a relationship that you want to commit to; (2) provide advice on what to focus on now if you feel ready to date and you want to take the next step.

I have included some of my clients' dating stories (obviously with their permission). They are all true, and I don't doubt that many will make you burst with laughter—or even make you cry. Finding Mr. Right is like Indiana Jones finding the holy grail.

1.
THE FIRST DATE AND YOUR NEW POWER TEAM:

Me, the Police, Fire and Ambulance Service.

Men are and will always be visual when it comes to deciding what they want. They make their minds up within thirty seconds if they fancy you, so yes—what you've always wondered is true. I'm afraid it's all about looks; always dress to impress on a first date.

If you've ever been on one, you'll know that the first date is always nerve-racking, and it's tempting to open the wine. But hear this: Most men find drunk women a massive turn-off, so settle your nerves, by all means, but always be in control.

I'm going to tell you a story from a young lady I looked after that should be remembered at all costs!

This young girl was going on a first date, and she was excruciatingly nervous, which is totally understandable. While she was getting ready, she didn't want to eat so that her stomach would be nice and flat in her dress. Big mistake! Getting ready, the nerves were starting to kick in big time. She opened a bottle of wine, and had a couple of glasses to calm her nerves.

She was all ready to go and meet her date. They really hit it off. She said he really seemed to be into her. They ordered a bottle of wine and both had a couple of glasses. The waiter brought out their starter, a very small prawn cocktail which she can't remember if it was nice or not. Then they had to wait over thirty minutes or more for their main course, so her date ordered another bottle of wine. She was starting to feel light headed, but didn't say anything, and by the time they brought the main meal out, she'd had nearly two bottles of wine. She rose from the table and threw up all over the table and down her dress. The staff had to help her to the toilet.

Her date was great. He got her home in a taxi and stayed with her to drop her off. The next day she was mortified and couldn't believe he wanted to see her again. She was very lucky as he might not have been that nice and caring.

Ladies, if you do worry about your stomach, you can get the right underwear to hold your stomach in under a dress, or you can shop for a shift dress as a lot of those dresses are cut well. They generally have a panel that can hide your stomach, but make sure you eat while you drink, and follow my tips below if you are nervous.

For sure you will be feeling nervous. You need to have the right mindset so you ooze confidence. Before reading any further I want you to visualize a team of people from different backgrounds that inspire you. Do the following exercise:

Create your power team. What I mean by this is imagine a team of people who inspire you; now visualize yourself as one of them—for instance, if you need to feel sexy, then have someone on your team who you feel is sexy.

For example:

Sexy: Pamela Anderson, Marilyn Monroe, Eva Mendes (How would Pamela, Eva or Marilyn come across on a date?)

Confident: Alesha Dixon, Beyoncé, Meghan Markle, Susannah Reid, Holly Willoughby, Davina McCall

Intelligent and Strong: Oprah Winfrey, Karen Brady, Sheryl Kara Sandberg

Funny and Confident: Jennifer Aniston, Amy Schumer, Kelly Brook

Who do you think is ultra-confident? I personally think Amanda Holden is a great example, or Cameron Diaz. Both are mature, gorgeous women who always present themselves well and know how to make an impact in every room they go into. Were they always like this? No; they had vulnerabilities when they were younger like everyone else.

Now ask yourself this: How would Amanda or Cameron make an entrance? Would these ladies hold their heads high, give direct eye contact, smile and walk with swagger? You know that they would, and you need to rehearse doing the same; practice until it becomes a habit.

I'm not saying change your personality, but just visualize yourself as someone like Amanda or Cameron. Tip: Think about your ideal role model for this exercise. Practice a few times on friends before you go out so you're feeling more confident. It may feel embarrassing at first, but you are better off stumbling in front of a best friend than your date.

It's best not to treat the date like a date. Think of it as your meeting a new friend. It tones down your nerves, and it's exciting because you may end up having a new friend for life. If not, just take what you can from that experience. What did you enjoy? What didn't you like? What have you learnt about yourself on this date? What would you change next time? Don't forget to praise yourself for doing so well for going out on a date with a stranger. It's not as easy as it sounds, and you should be proud of yourself. You go, girl!

Tip: Always be prepared; if you're on a first date and don't like him, have excuses at the ready. You need to have a passcode prepared, like the word "fridge."

Tell your girlfriend or relative that you are on a date and get them to call you thirty minutes into it. Prepare them in advance if you need to use the passcode (*fridge*) you've told them about; then your friend knows to call back and say there's been an emergency. Put them on loudspeaker so you're in no danger of leaving the date feeling embarrassed that you do not like them, and you want to leave. It's undoubtedly the easiest way to avoid that awkward goodbye on an early exit.

Very important: security. Make sure when you go on a first date, you do not go back to his place. Stats show risk of rape is at its highest when females on first dates go to a man's home. Always have a taxi booked at a set time or have a friend or family member pick you up, and make sure he knows.

Now, before I share some true incredible client stories, let's start close to home: ME! I don't think you can top it, but if you can, please, let me know. I would love to hear your stories.

You'll read a few crazy stories in this book. Just remember this as the one where I ended up with the police, fire service and an ambulance, and I had only been out for an hour and a half.

So, there I was in my prime and aged twenty-six! The date was set and so exciting. The guy had put in so much effort. We went to a lovely restaurant for a swanky dinner, and yes, believe it or not, I only had one glass of wine. So, I was on my best behavior—well, trying to be, at least! I spent half the day shopping for a new outfit, and hours to get ready and feel good. I felt like a million dollars as I left my house.

We had gone to a fishing village, called Pevensey Bay. It was a stunning evening in late summer, so we thought we would have a romantic stroll along to Pevensey Castle. Unfortunately, on arrival, I had an idea that might not have been one of my best. This idiot—moi—decided to be nosey and climb on top of the wall to see if we could have a peek at the castle, which sat behind the wall. Sounds like a good idea, right? What could possibly go wrong?

As I attempted to straddle the wall, I slipped and fell close to twenty feet. It was a little bit like Del Boy in *Only Fools and Horses* when he falls through the bar flap, if you have ever seen the episode (series 6 episode 1, "Yuppy Love"). As people say, you could not have made it up!!

I was mortified, embarrassed and very, very sore. The police turned up with the fire brigade and an ambulance. Then the firemen were sent down to help the ambulance men to get me on a stretcher and pull me out with the fire engine. (No, I am not that big a unit! I was a long way down!)

I wanted the ground to just swallow me up there and then. But the police needed to ask me a few questions. . .

"Miss Palmer, this castle has been here since 1066, built by William the Conqueror to keep people out, and no one to our knowledge has ever fallen down. How long have you been down there?"

For once in my life, I was stunned into silence. I hadn't even been there two hours. Next thing I knew, I had to go in the ambulance for X-rays at the hospital.

I was very lucky—a ruined outfit, a few bruises, ego crushed, and, you guessed it, I didn't see the guy again, although he seemed a lovely man! Ladies, best tip: Always wear good underwear when you go abseiling.

So, first dates can be fun. If I didn't go, this would never have happened, and at least the story always makes people laugh!

Who knows what's going to happen on your first date? Just don't be nosey like me if you can help it! On the plus side of my embarrassing experience, I did get to see some rather tasty firemen, so no complaints there.

So, back to the first date. Many people ask me what to do at the awkward part when the dreaded bill comes.

Men are funny creatures (plenty of my clients have other not-so-funny names for them). The best thing you can do is always offer to buy them a drink at the start of the date. It's a psychological thing. Most men will say no; nearly all will be prepared to pay for dinner. Worst case, ladies, and do be prepared—you might need to go Dutch. Embarrassing, but you might need to split the bill.

Call me old fashioned, but most men don't realize how much you have spent for the bloody date in the first place. New underwear, manicure, new outfit, then the hours of getting ready. All of that takes time and a lot of money! There's no doubt about it—the man should always pay the bill. Not only does it show you that he's a true gent and will look after you, but also when and if you have children, the chances are he will be a generous and supportive father.

If you go out to dinner, eat sexily, take your time, be seductive. If this feels unnatural, get the wine out and practice with a girlfriend. I promise you it will be a giggle, but it will help.

Getting the salad on the date when really you want a burger and chips is a bullet that you just have to bite. Girls, in the past if you saw me after a date when I got home, you would see me stuffing myself silly with chocolate biscuits!

What you need to do at the start when he is watching you is to seduce him whilst eating. Maybe when you're eating a breadstick, caress it with your mouth. You know he will be imagining you caressing and licking something else!! Remember, belly, ego and. . .

Talking about first dates, let me tell you a story about one of my male clients I introduced to one of my female clients. It's hilarious; now it's the main story at all of his dinner parties.

"My mess at the mansion got me literally dumped"

A client of mine has IBS. It's horrible for him, but he copes as well with it as anyone can. A couple of years ago he went for a date quite soon after meeting this girl who was very wealthy and, in his words, stunning.

When she invited him to her beautiful home, he knew that he was going to have to really dress to impress and act the part. As he predicted, it was an incredible house, and he was almost too scared to touch anything. The place was immaculate.

He was also quite nervous, so he told her he needed the loo. Unfortunately, one of the main symptoms of IBS is the possibility of loose bowels in anxious situations, so he expected that he might need the toilet at some point. He had learned over the years to control it, but he knew in that moment he was in trouble.

Whilst rushing to the toilet, disaster struck. All of a sudden, he had an uncontrollable bowel movement. He could feel that it had gone horribly wrong; he knew he was in trouble and urgently needed to get to the toilet to clean himself up.

He was frantic, and because the house was so huge, he got lost on his way back from the bathroom. Panicking like mad upstairs, he wasn't thinking straight and made a bizarre decision—to throw his underwear out of the front window, thinking he would try and pick them up when he left as he didn't want to walk back downstairs with the smelly pants. Sounds like a good plan? No!

It didn't work out that way. He was mortified to discover that he didn't throw them out of the front of the house, but out of the back of the house and on top of the conservatory roof. They were lodged there and beyond retrieval. So, the soiled, stinking pants stayed there—and guess what? He never heard from or saw her again!!

My motto to this story is to try to relax! We all get tense on dates, and if we like the person, we can get ourselves tied up in knots. But honestly, it does us no good at all. Before you go and meet someone you really like, or put yourself in a nerve-racking situation, take some time out before you arrive to just chill out. Think about your confidence team. Who are you going to imagine you are? Have some quiet time and mentally prepare for what is about to happen. You are strong and can cope with anything. Just believe in yourself! And if you are a guy reading this, take spare pants!

Notes:

2.
MAKEUP FOR A FIRST DATE AND WHAT TO WEAR

As I've said, men are visual creatures, so always dress to impress; that means classy and sexy but not slutty. Think about what sort of date you are going on and dress appropriately.

In my business it's vital to have the right contacts and know the right people. I work globally with some of the leading experts in their respective fields. I'm very lucky to work with one of the top UK celebrity makeup artists, who has worked with the likes of Pamela Anderson.

Estelle has given me her top seven tips to share with you.

1. Start by prepping your skin the night before to give you a lovely, healthy glow. Buy a moisturizing face mask or make a homemade one of Greek yogurt and honey. It's great for giving the skin a boost! Warning, though; don't ever use a clarifying mask or cleansing mask the night before. This could result in red blemishes the next day!

2. Less is more. Make the most of your best features with your makeup, but don't overdo it. When asked, most men like women with natural makeup as opposed to heavy overdone looks. When a man is hopefully gazing into your eyes, you don't want his first thought to be how much mascara you've used!!

3. Start with a good coverage foundation that looks light on the skin. A good way to do this is by literally only using it where there are imperfections and leaving the rest of the skin free. This gives a wonderful natural look.

4. If you want to go for a sexy red lip, balance it out by playing the eyes down, either with a soft eyeshadow or simple slick of eyeliner.

5. Don't try new hairstyles that you haven't previously tested out. Keep it simple and wear your hair the way that most feels like you. Freshly washed hair with a spritz of perfume over is perfect!

6. Give a little bit of attention to your nails. If you don't have time for a manicure, make sure they're as tidy as they can be as they'll be noticed if you're holding a wineglass or eating.

7. Give those hands an extra treat and moisturize several times the night before, whilst your face mask is on maybe!

Now your outfit for your date: Choose a dress that shows your chest and neckline so that he can see enough to get excited and keen. But it's important also not to flaunt your assets too much as in the back of his mind he will be thinking, *Is she wife material? Can I take her home to my mum? Would she be a good mother to my children?* Silly, I know, but it's a proven fact: this is how most men think. That being said, I will mention "whores" and "Mary Poppinses" later!

Heels are great as they give you an hourglass figure. Nearly all men love heels; it's best to get a heel that's open so you have more leg on show. Men adore legs and bums, but check his height and do not dwarf him. Tip: Most men don't like to be towered over, so careful on the heels; try and find out your date's height in advance.

Talking of heels, I'm going to tell you another funny story, which happened to a female client.

This lady was in her late twenties, and she met this really nice guy in a wine bar. They got on really well, and both decided to meet up again. He said he would pick her up and take her out for dinner. As luck would have it, he only lived five minutes away from her. He was really excited as he was picking up his new blue BMW car.

The day arrived for their date, and he arrived to pick her up, but he was fifteen minutes early.

"Why do they have to turn up early when you don't want them too?" she lamented to me. Typical! He rang the doorbell, and she looked out and saw him and his new shiny car.

She was still getting ready and trying to hurry up! She rushed outside as it started to get dusky. She couldn't see too well, and the grass was wet, and it was getting cold. She ran out across the grass, not looking at the ground; she was staring at her date, smiling and excited. She got into the car and kissed him on the cheek to say hello. All of a sudden, there was a terrible smell. She looked down and saw that she had stepped in dog muck; it was all over his new carpet! She wanted the ground to swallow her up. She was super embarrassed. Turning to him she saw he had a face like thunder; he was not impressed! She ran back indoors to clean up. As you can imagine, it was not a good way to start a new relationship. The good news is even to this day they still laugh about it!

Tip, ladies: Tell them not to be early! Never run, never look too eager!

So that's your shoes looked after. Now, ladies, we all know boobs are a no-brainer as men love them! So, invest in a great bra that pulls your breasts together but doesn't put them fully on display.

Lastly, your bum; it's important to dress depending on your figure. Tip: Pick a dress that nips you in at the waistline and shows your beautiful curves. Curves are a winner as men love curves and bums, so flaunt them and be proud.

Notes:

3.
HOW TO FLIRT

The Lady and the Guy with the Humongous Balls.

Flirting. It's simple, really, because it's all about eye contact, lips, mouth, hair, touch and being fun and having a winning smile. I will explain more shortly, but first a couple of funny stories.

This has to be the best icebreaker ever. One of my best friends, many years ago before she got married, always used to take a golf ball with her on a girls' night out. If she fancied someone, she would walk up behind them, nudge them, and when they looked, she would say with a big smile on her face, "Have you dropped your balls?" She never failed to get a laugh, and as she is a good-looking girl, if the guy was single, she was often set for the night. She got quite a lot of phone numbers! This might not be for you, but it's bloody funny and it works!

Talking of balls, I must tell you this about one of my clients.

The Lady and the Guy with the Humongous Balls

I have this one client who is hilarious, loves dating, is great fun to be around, and a real flirt—you might say the life and soul of the party. I set her up with a guy the year before last who she went out with a few times and really liked. After a few weeks, one thing led to another, and they ended up naked in the bedroom.

She rang me the following day and could not stop laughing. I asked what was wrong. She then went on to describe his penis, which was OK, she said, but apparently he had enormous (her words) saggy balls, which had me in stitches. She made an off-the-cuff remark—"They should invent a clip or band to pull them together"—which again caused me to double over laughing.

Two weeks later I was out with the same lady and three other clients, and we had the funniest lunch ever. As you can imagine, the saggy balls were the topic of conversation, but interestingly two of the other ladies had similar experiences!!

The moral of the story is accept people for their wobbly bits, or keep the lights off when you are in the bedroom. BTW, she never saw him again.

Back to flirting: Your mouth and lips are a very important part of flirting. Seductively and casually bite and lick your lips and think sexy! (Use your power team.)

This is important when flirting. It's all about making the person you're with feel like they are the center of attention. Laugh and smile lots. Be chatty as this will really help to make him feel good about the date and he will feel relaxed. He will know you are enjoying his company.

Men are generally more scared and nervous than you. Most men won't ask someone out on a date or chat them up for fear of rejection.

When your date is talking to you, always look deeply into his eyes and keep good eye contact. Repeat some of the phrases he is saying, as this will give him the knowledge that you are taking in everything he is telling you, and he will know and feel that you are really into him.

When you are on a date and when you want to go to the toilet, push your chest out while getting up from the table, then lower yourself slowly, get your bag from the floor, flash some leg and your booty. Swish your hair and be damn seductive. Trust me, he will be looking.

Tip: Use your team to be Pamela or Eva and, in that moment, imagine you are her! He will be massively turned on, and you will be guaranteed to get that text message or call for the second date.

Tip: One of the biggest qualities men look for in a woman is confidence! (Use your team.)

Men need their ego fed. You will need to say how good he looks, what a great smile he has, and comment on his great physique and any other attributes he is genuinely blessed with!

For example, you can say, "You look really hot in that shirt." If you are sat opposite him, visually run your eyeline down his chest and smile. If you are next to him, slowly lean into him and run your hand down his shirt. He'll know you're a flirt and tease, but he will love it.

After that, back off a little, as you don't want to come across too eager! Be brave—controlled, but brave.

How to test whether he likes you: This sounds crazy, but try this at the end of the date. It always works. Accidentally bump into him when you're leaving, let him rescue you, get close, look directly into his eyes, and hold the stare for a split second and smile. It will definitely make him giddy, and he will see you are playful and fun. Men love to be a hero!

Tip: You need to say his name in conversation. Men love to hear it said out loud by the opposite sex. Strange but true! Ladies if you are applying this in the bedroom, make sure you get his name right!

Tip: If he is really hot and you really are getting on well, maybe try and feed him. Men love the attention. It strokes their EGO.

Tip: Remember, the guy may not be Mr. Right, but he could become a great friend. Enjoy his company if you can. Whatever the outcome, be nice.

I'm going to tell you a story about one of my clients who is probably the best at flirting I have ever witnessed. She also believes she can read any man, but was she ever in for a surprise!

"He was a fun-gi [guy] to be with, until. . . "

So, my wonderful client, very attractive with a great personality, was very unlucky when it comes to men. I am pleased to say I have now introduced her to Mr. Right.

Before she met Mr. Right, she'd met this guy and loved his sparkling personality. Two or three weeks of perfect dating passed; he was the ultimate gentleman. He made her laugh and was clever.

Now, remember, this lady is an expert at flirting and thinks she can read any man!

What could go wrong, you must be thinking?

Well, around the three-week mark, the big night of passion arrived. She knew now was the time and he'd no doubt lived up to the high bar he'd set himself in all other areas.

Everything was wonderful, until she unzipped his trousers and was about to take the next steps.

As she felt around the crotch area, she *finally* found what she was aiming for—but the truth was, she had to search for it.

When she was brave enough to look down, she saw a small penis, which she described as a button mushroom. She said it was less than two inches big, and that was probably being generous. It was skinny and round at the end. She said it was exactly like the kind of knobbly little thing you'd find in the vegetable aisle at the supermarket.

She wasn't just embarrassed; she was upset too. "I loved being with the guy. I can't fault anything about him—but I can't be with someone with a penis that small and strange for the rest of my life."

The next day, she reluctantly ended it, feeling guilty about her reason, but also knowing that she had to be true to herself.

My motto for this story is, and you might have heard the saying as a joke, but I'm afraid to say it's true, *Check out the goods before you take them home. I don't mean just touch them; have a sneaky peek at his trousers!*

Notes:

4.
DATING AND FINDING COMMON GROUND AND THINGS YOU BOTH ENJOY

The Story of "A Wee-ly Nice Bloke, but It All Went Wrong."

Men like to talk about themselves, as we all do! So do try and find common ground—perhaps something you both do at work, hobbies, maybe holidays or things you like doing that are the same. Here are some things you may have in common:

- Job/work
- Food
- Health and Fitness
- Music
- Family
- Hobbies
- Accomplishments
- Goals
- Animals/Pets
- Favorite Films/ TV shows
- Charity
- Property

- Politics
- Holidays
- Studies

If you have pets, that can be a good starting point as an icebreaker. People love to chat about their pets. Remember, everyone has interests; you need to find his like your life depends on it!

Task: Make a list of all the things he likes and especially focus on the ones you know little or nothing about; then go out of your way to learn something about whatever it is. He will be amazed that you have such a wide knowledge on the things he enjoys doing.

A great question to ask is "Where do you like to go on holiday and what do you like to do?" This way, you will get to know exactly what he's like. He may say he wants to relax, party or be a beach bum. Maybe he sees himself as an explorer; these things are all valuable to know, so you know who and what you are dealing with.

Another excellent icebreaker is "What's the most embarrassing thing that's happened to you?" This will make you both laugh, and laughter is key. Make sure you have something ready to tell him, but never lie about anything! It always comes back to bite you on the bum.

Then there's the question "What's on your bucket list?" This will help you find some common ground quickly, maybe even lead towards a next date. If he says he wants to go in a hot air balloon and perhaps you do too, it's something amazing you can experience together that instantly becomes an important shared memory.

Another is "Do you have any party tricks?" This one can be funny and entertaining. Have one up your sleeve. In fact, if you like, you can use mine. Just tell him that you know how to hypnotize chickens—and if you contact me, I promise that I will teach you for free! (Ask Simon Cowell.) My nan used to keep chickens, and she taught me this trick as a young girl. This party trick is hilarious.

Then there is the goodbye on the first date. Awkward? No, it does not need to be. If you like him, smile, and tell him you had a great time, and it was fun, and it would be good to see him again. The next move is yours. Kiss his cheek or lips, but this is a peck; keep him wanting more.

Make sure you've got the breath freshener or the gum in your bag ready to use.

Tip: If you are really getting on like a house on fire and you can tell he wants to kiss you properly, go for it; lock lips. You could be onto a winner.

Finally, let him text you. If he wants you, I promise you he will call or text you; otherwise, it just wasn't meant to be! When he contacts you, my advice is to always message him back within an hour. That way he knows you are keen, which is great because so is he!

But whatever you do, don't leave him hanging around. Try to give him a flirty and positive message back. Something like "I had a really great night, handsome. You really did make me laugh," but only send this if he has texted you first. Tip: It's a dating rule to live by.

Sometimes the dating goes great and there is lots of common ground until. . .

"A wee-ly nice bloke, but it all went wrong."

One woman I've worked with had been on a few dates with a really nice guy. They got on well and found that they had a lot in common too. One night, they went to a party together and had a great time, so she invited him back to stay over. After a fantastic romp in the bedroom, they both went to sleep with a warm glow about them.

But that wasn't the only warm thing she would feel in bed. In the middle of the night, she suddenly woke up. After feeling something strange had happened, she examined herself—only to find out that she was soaking wet.

He had urinated—directly all over her. The smell was rancid. Unfortunately, he was so embarrassed and never phoned her again. Maybe some things *are* too good to be true!

My motto for this story is that, hey, we are all human at the end of the day. Your partner must accept you for your flaws too as no one is perfect. If something embarrassing happens, you don't have to let it ruin the relationship.

Communication is the key; if the other person fails to understand, then they are not the one for you.

Notes:

5.
WHAT TO SAY ON A DATE AND THE RIGHT BODY LANGUAGE; CONFIDENCE AND HOW TO TELL HE IS BEING TRUTHFUL

"My New Hubby Had No Penis"

B efore we start, I need to tell you a really sad story that happened to a client. In life and especially in relationships, you really need to be truthful, as otherwise it will end in tears!

"My new hubby had no penis"

Once, I had a client who had met her partner and fell in love, quickly got engaged, and couldn't have been any happier.

However, her religion stopped her from having sex before marriage. Although this may seem like a very old-fashioned value to most of us, a lot of women still believe in this principle, and it's something to be accepted by all.

So, as you can imagine, on her wedding night she was so excited about losing her virginity to the man she truly loved. After a beautiful day and bidding their guests farewell, off they went to their room.

Then, unexpectedly, he sat her down and said, "I have something I need to tell you." Hoping that it would be some kind of wonderful treat he had meticulously planned, she waited with bated breath, but suddenly the mood dropped—and she felt it would be something bad.

"Darling, I have a birth defect which means I have no penis," he said woefully. It won't shock you to hear that this crushed her. Not only would it impact their intimacy, but she had planned her whole marriage around having children. She felt betrayed and lied to for the year they were together before the wedding. She eventually left him, but it took her years to recover from the huge letdown. Luckily, she was still young and in her twenties—and she found love again, along with a proper sex life!

My motto of this story is never lie! Honesty is always the best policy. You run the risk of ruining everything because, eventually, the truth is always revealed.

Now, back to lies, confidence and body language. I suppose you could say that my line of work is pretty different to your average nine-to-five, but just as in any industry, it's vital to have the right contacts and know the right people. We all have invaluable experience to share, and by helping others, we also build trusted friendships that last forever.

Take Darren for example; Darren Stanton is the UK's TV body-language expert and human lie detector. He's always given me brilliant advice on how my clients can present the physical side of themselves to get the optimum effect.

This is something that Darren told me that I want to share with you: "The easiest way to build rapport and a connection with another person, especially on a date, is what experts call matching and mirroring," he says. "This means that you simply match the body language of the other person in terms of what they do with their hands, how they fit. If standing, are they standing on both feet or with weight on one foot over the other? All of this stuff counts.

"As you talk to them, after a few minutes of conversation if you subtly change something small about your body language—for example, if they had their arms crossed and you matched them, you might like to uncross your arms and see if they do the same. The simple answer is that if they do, this means they feel relaxed and connect with you."

This was all a revelation to me. Who knew you could learn so much about someone by just watching tiny gestures of their body and using the same gestures to give them the same subliminal messages?

Something I had always wondered about was how much eye contact to give on a date. Surely you can give too much—and possibly not enough too? Darren's opinion on this is fascinating.

He says, "Normally eye contact is about three to five seconds before a person begins to feel uncomfortable and needs to break contact for a second or two. If the person you are talking to is happy to maintain eye contact beyond the five second period, then that is another great sign that they are into you and attraction is growing."

There was something else I needed to know. It was the burning question that I've always wanted the answer to—how about being able to tell when someone is potentially lying to you?

Darren told me straight, "Well, telling a lie to avoid social awkwardness is quite normal. For example, telling someone that the birthday present they just brought to you is fantastic when you really think it is terrible is quite normal.

"Generally, people tend to tell darker lies in an attempt to manipulate you into saying or doing something that they want. If the other person is trying to tell you something like 'I did not cheat on you,' then they will forget things like their normal hand gestures—and ways of sitting and speaking.

"They will also overcompensate the amount of eye contact they usually give you because they are trying to convince you they are being truthful. It's more commonly regarded that a liar cannot look you in the eye.

"Listen too for what they say as well as what they do; sarcasm is very often a good indicator as to whether someone is being truthful with you or not."

What I learned from Darren has been invaluable—in life, and not just dating. To accuse someone of being a liar is a big move. Therefore, you need to use great caution with your thinking and how the words come out of your mouth. It's important to remember that most people are honest—but there are some bad apples out there too.

I'm so grateful to have a friend like Darren, and I fully intend to keep my ears open and always be improving my knowledge about what makes people tick. It helps my clients and me too, so a no-brainer, really.

A few years ago, one of my male clients met a gorgeous woman who was too good to be true.

She was quite literally drop-dead gorgeous—a blonde with long, shapely legs and the perfect bum to match.

After two dates, he was keen to take things a little further, and on their second night out, things started to heat up when they got back to her place.

With her hourglass figure and perfect breasts, he just couldn't get enough of her. As the passion progressed, he began kissing her all over and went to kiss her down below. When he began to sensually touch her, he couldn't help but think what a strangely shaped vagina she had . . . Something just didn't seem right.

It then became apparent that this stunning lady he'd been falling for was a "he." And my startled client made a sharp exit.

The moral of this story is if things seem too good to be true, always go with your gut feeling; nine times out of ten, you will be right!

Notes:

6.
WHAT MEN REALLY WANT AND HOW TO KEEP HIM

Mary Poppins and the Whore

A motto I like to live by is "Be like an onion; slowly keep revealing more layers and always leave him wanting more." It's a great way to keep the spark alive in every way.

If you really want to keep the guy, then be mindful not to criticize him too much. Men need their ego stroked daily, to feel good and wanted. Don't overdo it, though; about one or two ego boosts a day are enough for any man! Also, don't be a pushover, as men love the chase. Make him work to get you and keep you.

Laugh at what he says (even if it's not bloody funny). But whatever you do, don't talk about your problems to him if you have just started dating. He is working you out like you are working him out. Keep the conversation light hearted, friendly, and above all else fun. If you have some challenges in your life, leave that stuff for your girlfriends until you are confident of this man.

Men are not always the best communicators, and often won't ask you for a cuddle or a kiss, but men need and want to feel loved, appreciated and respected, so don't forget this. Give him a small daily dose, but don't overdo it. He will appreciate it.

Men do like alone time, so go out with girlfriends once a week or every two weeks. This will give him time to miss you and be thinking about you. If he doesn't like you going out, you have a problem. This must be dealt with really early, ladies. Remember, kill monsters when they are small!! Do not let this grow into a big problem where you end up being downtrodden.

Trust is a big thing. Don't ask him every day what he is up to and where he is going. In my experience, more often than not he will tell you anyway, but if you're constantly checking on him, he will start to feel trapped. So, don't smother him!

The best relationships are built on mutual trust and respect for each other. Things are not one sided, and you both need to communicate well.

Men were put on this earth to provide and protect; that's the way they are programmed. When he offers to help, let him. He wants to feel like a man!

Let him lead, as men want to feel like leaders. Being able to do this gives him a good feeling in the relationship, as he might not be a leader in his job, so let him have the chance to be a leader. You want a happy, content man. This will make him feel good and release the endorphins!

Tip: This may sound harder than it is, but you need to think about the fact that you really need to be two people—a whore in the bedroom, and Mary Poppins in all the other rooms! A bit of a contrast, I'm sure you'll agree—but believe me, that's what most men want.

Tip: Men like to feel masculine, so make sure to express that you need him to put a shelf up or kill a spider. It may sound corny, but whilst he's doing that, tell him something like, "You're so brave; it turns me on seeing your muscles and sexy bum putting up that shelf." Don't be too needy. It's easy, though, to make him feel as if you need him so he feels secure. It's also a bit of fun.

Tip: Men don't always understand women. There have been many books written on the subject. Most men don't like too much detail, so when you are explaining something or you have a problem, keep it short and to the point, but make sure you have an outcome so that he knows you need his help. Generally, men are very good at finding solutions. Try not to ask when he is too busy with work or in a bad mood, as they can't cope with too much at one time! LOL.

Notes:

7.
WHAT TO DO TO TURN HIM ON

1: Send flirty text messages when you feel the time is right; you can say far more to him and get to know his sexual preferences by using text messages. He will be so into you. Test his boundaries. Be daring. If he fancies you, he will be longing to have sex with you. (Ladies, do NOT send raunchy photos.)

2: Ask him! You never know what he will come out with!

3: If you are into sex toys, introduce him to them. Most men enjoy fun in the bedroom. If you both are not experienced, give it a go. Relax and have fun.

4: If you both enjoy watching adult films, indulge and watch them together.

5: Silky sexy underwear is a must. I personally feel sexy in underwear. Again, a pretty bra and sexy knickers that cover your body parts is far more of a turn-on.

6. When you're out, whisper in his ear, talk slowly and quietly, lick and bite around his ear—although be careful not to nibble too much. We don't want a trip to the emergency room.

7. The more you kiss, touch and feel his upper body, the more endorphins he will release. It will boost his feeling of intimacy.

8. Talk dirty to him in the bedroom. Most men enjoy it. Start slowly to check if he does, and if you get the right signals, have fun together, laugh and carry on.

9. Nearly all men want a woman that they feel they can trust, is a great homemaker, has ambition, and is great at hosting friends and family. If any of these are weaknesses, you must work on making them strengths.

10. Money permitting, book weekends or nights away and don't tell him you are going. Throughout the days give him clues; let him know he is in for a real treat.

Question: How long should you wait to have sex?

This is a question I get asked all the time. The answer is "as long as possible." Try and make him wait, as that will drive him crazy. You also want him to trust you so he knows that when you go out at night with a friend, you won't be playing around with anyone else. So, if you can make him wait a month, it will be worth it. Ladies, you already know ways of keeping him happy without full-blown sex. Give him a taste of things to come.

Notes:

8.
HOW TO MAKE A MAN HAPPY

The Story of the Lady "Who Would Rather Cut Off Her Right Toe Than Give Him Another Blow Job!"

Remember, belly, ego and _____—and where possible, try and get some fun hobbies you both enjoy!

1: Be great in bed; make sure he knows what you like, and you know what he likes.

2: Talk to him. Most men seem full of confidence, but in my experience, many are insecure. Make sure he knows he can talk to you about anything; you are his best friend.

3: If you don't like his hobbies, learn to give him the space to enjoy them. We all need time to unwind.

4: Buy killer underwear, keep fit and have bags of energy.

5: Be nice to his best friends, family, especially his mum. (Even if you don't get on, it's very difficult for him try to live in harmony if you don't.) Remember, you may only see them every now and then, so if things are challenging, try and bite your lip.

6: Be a great hostess (even if you can't/don't cook).

7: Dress well when you need to; when you don't, be comfortable, but cute-and-sexy comfortable; perhaps just his T-shirt—simple, but very sexy.

8: If you can, once a week run a bath that you can both enjoy;

that way you can both relax together with no distractions. Put the music on and get the candles out, a bottle of bubbles, and enjoy quality time together!

9: Men, believe it or not, want to make you happy! If he sees you happy, he's happy. If he sees you are not happy, he will start to be concerned, and more often than not he will think he has upset you. If and when you are unhappy, learn to be a great communicator. Men are simple creatures. They just want to know where they stand and what to do next!!

10. At the start of a new relationship, if a man gives you a gift, don't reject it, as it pushes him away. Allow him to carry your bag or open the door. It makes him feel good, as men were put on this earth to provide and protect, and they need to feel they are doing that.

Talking about the need to connect and how to make a man happy, here is a funny story! One of my clients from years ago said to me, and I quote, "Lisa, I would rather cut off my right toe than give him another blow job!"

There is no getting away from it; the fact is that men love blow jobs, especially when it's a new relationship. My client said she "doesn't mind that much, but after a while, quite frankly it's bloody boring. Added to which, it gives you the worst mouth-and-jaw ache! In fact, a friend of mine only gives one to her hubby when she wants something!"

Now, ladies, as you well know, the worst thing ever is when men are ill. They are an absolute pain in the arse, like no one has ever been as ill as them. Yeah right! Honestly! It's like looking after a baby. If your man has man-flu, make him feel special by cooking him good hearty food and letting him have the remote control—even if *Love Island* is on; just put it on record for when he gets better. Thank God for catch-up TV!

Food is very important; to keep that belly full is a must!

As I said earlier, one of the ways to a man's heart is through his stomach. I hope you're not like me because I could burn hot water. I'm a bloody awful cook, so if you're similar, get some lessons!

Just learn the basics, like cooking pasta or shepherd's pie.

The best and easiest thing to cook is usually meat. No matter what they say, most men are still cavemen. Yes, I know all those feminists out there will have something to say about a statement like this, but men are men at the end of the day.

I got some great tips from celebrity chef Rosemary Shrager a few years ago when we did a TV show together. The best tip was how to cook a steak in minutes! Rosemary says firstly you get the pan and the oil extremely hot. You then get your steak and bash it so it tenderizes the meat, which makes it taste better. After that, you cook it for a few minutes whilst turning it over each side, then serve with chips, peas and peppercorn sauce. It's an easy and quick dinner to prepare if you are cooking for the evening, which gives you more time to get ready. Give it a go.

Seriously, if you do hate cooking, just get great at five main meals, write down the recipes and keep them safe and follow the instructions. Please note: Stay in the kitchen and concentrate; otherwise, you will burn everything!

Notes:

9.
STALE RELATIONSHIPS

How to Bring Back the Fun and Keep the Romance Alive

Remember what I said at the start of the book? We love men, but sometimes things go stale, and we must take action.

Feel you've lost your spark? Do you need to, in the words of Take That, "Relight Your Fire"?

I see so many unhappy clients who feel they have lost the spark and aren't sure where to turn. Many couples give up too easily these days, with divorce rates at thirteen couples an hour. A shocking statistic.

It is so easy to fall into a routine and lose the motivation to go out and experience new things together. We've all been in a long-term relationship or married to an old grumpy git and thought, *Where the hell did the fun go*, right?

Friday nights have inevitably become the same unexciting sequence of dull events as you both sit at home watching *EastEnders*, whilst he farts and flicks through endless television channels before falling asleep on the sofa. You can imagine it now: He's slumped over and attractively (not) catching flies and heavily breathing out the garlic bread you had for dinner. It's certainly not an image of Brad Pitt!

If you're reading this and have forgotten what decent sex life is, it's time to take action.

Maybe it has got to the stage that you find more excitement through consuming a bar of Cadburys than making the effort to have sex at the end of a fun-filled, TV-fueled night in. Yawn!

My advice? Try alpha-dating! This is a way to put the excitement, mystery and fun back into your relationship by going week by week (or month by month) and taking it in turns to go through the alphabet, coming up with a different date beginning with each letter of the alphabet.

For example, *A* could be for *archery*; and you can go and have a giggle and a day out.

And it doesn't have to always be an adventure. It can be something different in the bedroom—or going to a new location for a romantic night away. This method adds an element of surprise and creates something you can both look forward to. Use your creativity and make it personal to you both.

A: Ascot Racecourse; cheeky day and night away, which will be fun.

B: Brighton seaside stroll along the beach, hand in hand, sharing a bag of chips!

C: C**k ring; try something new in the bedroom. This is a great toy for you both.

So many relationships break down as they lack the three elements that are key to a successful and long-lasting bond: FUN, INTIMACY and COMMUNICATION.

Get these three well balanced, and you should stay happy in your relationship.

We all want that first-date feeling back, the element of surprise and those jittering butterflies in your tummy. So, don't sit around; get out there and create new memories. Give yourselves new things to chat and joke about, and all in all get back to enjoying each other's company.

Have fun with it; wind each other up, play games, give each other a clue or send a few saucy pictures! Times have changed, and we all have to change with them. We all need to ditch the bog-standard "date night" that often never happens and hit the new, modern way of dating.

Last of all, life is like a book; one chapter is happy, and one is sad, but if you don't turn the page, you never know what the next chapter holds. Remember, when you meet the one, you could end up with him for the next forty years or more, so what are you waiting for? Go out and have fun!

Love, Lisa
X

ACKNOWLEDGMENTS

I would love to personally thank Lucinda Ellery for all your support. I really do appreciate it, and of course Jonathan, a.k.a. "the Vagina" WhatsApp group, for all the laughs we have, Jonathan being one of the most perfect men!

Tom, my one and only, I thank you for your help. You really mean the world to me! Love you trillions.

Anne, a.k.a. "the Oracle," thank you for all your great advice. Love you lots.

I thank my mum and dad for giving birth to a legend, LOL. Thank you for all your help over the years; love you both lots.

Alison Fullick, a.k.a. "AAA," for some great face pulling; really appreciate your time and help, and poor JJ for having to take the photos!

Patricia Whitson, for being a total legend and all your wonderful advice.

Bradley, for being the most awesome son a mum could have!

Endy Engel, for being an awesome photographer.

Tati Carpenter, makeup and hairstylist, thank you for doing a great job. You had your work cut out for you!

Estelle Horder, makeup artist to the stars, thanks for the great tips!

Darren Stanton: Thanks, Darren. As always, awesome advice.

Sally Windsor, thank you so much for all your help.

Jolie Louise Turner, thank you for the wonderful drawing of Mary Poppins.

Azim Sachedina, RIP my dear friend. I would love to dedicate my book to one of the loveliest, kindest and very funny men! Youuuuuu.

Lisa with Jilly Cooper.

Lisa with footballer Sir Trevor Brooking.

Lisa with boxer Frank Bruno.

Lisa with Anton Mosimann, Prince Charles' chef.

Lisa with the UK's Prime Minister's mum and dad, Stanley Johnson and Charlotte Johnson Wahl.

Lisa with BBC Radio 1's Chris Stark.

Lisa with Tony Hadley and Brandon Block.

Lisa with Kriss Akabusi, former Olympian TV presenter, and Alex Mytton from *Made in Chelsea*.

Lisa with famous footballers, Peter Shilton OBE and Sir Trevor Brooking, and famous jockey, Bob Champion.

Lisa with Michel Drappier, owner of Drappier Champagne.

Lisa with comedian Micky Flanagan.